101

Ways to

Boost

Your

Science

Skills

101
Ways to
Boost
Your
Science
Skills

by Robert Hirschfeld

illustrated by Aija Janums

SCHOLASTIC INC.

New York Toronto London Auckland Sydney
Mexico City New Delhi Hong Kong Buenos Aires

ISBN 0-439-69759-X

12 11 10 9 8 7 6 5 4 3   4 5 6 7 8 9/0

Printed in the U.S.A.   40

First Scholastic printing, September 2004

To Nancy,
my best teacher and inspiration
—R.H.

CONTENTS

Chapter 1

Why This Book Is for You, Even If You Don't Love Science

It seems like so many books start out by telling you why their subject matter is so great and why you should love studying it. We're going to start out by saying that, whether you love science or not, *you can do it!* And this book will help you.

But (you knew that was coming), you can enjoy science a lot more if you take time to think about why you have to study it. So let's start out like all those other books and talk, just for a minute, about why you study science (aside from the fact that you have to):

- *You love science.* You're planning to be a doctor or a scientist someday, so you want to learn all you can now. If that's you, you won't need any more convincing.
- *Science is for everyone.* Even if you plan to be a violinist, a movie star, or a firefighter,

you can bet there will come a time when understanding a science idea will help you in a real, practical way. Why do you think tightening a violin string makes the sound higher? How do movies get onto the screen anyway, and how do we see them? What causes different kinds of fires, and what is the best way to put them out? See what we mean?

• *Science is always changing.* Of all your school subjects, science is the one that changes the most. Every day scientists learn new, exciting ideas. Take dinosaurs, for example. Until very recently, everyone believed that these creatures were reptiles who died out because they couldn't adapt to changing conditions on Earth. But new discoveries tell scientists that dinosaurs were more like birds than reptiles, and that they probably died out because of some disastrous event—most likely an asteroid hitting Earth. And think about this: until about five hundred years ago, many people were absolutely sure that

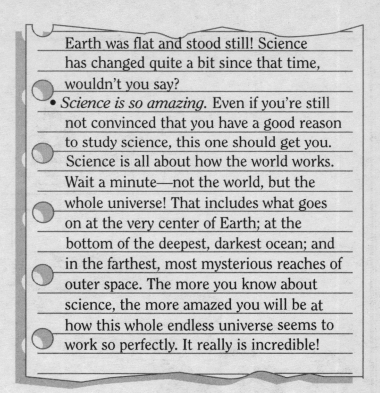

Earth was flat and stood still! Science has changed quite a bit since that time, wouldn't you say?

- *Science is so amazing.* Even if you're still not convinced that you have a good reason to study science, this one should get you. Science is all about how the world works. Wait a minute—not the world, but the whole universe! That includes what goes on at the very center of Earth; at the bottom of the deepest, darkest ocean; and in the farthest, most mysterious reaches of outer space. The more you know about science, the more amazed you will be at how this whole endless universe seems to work so perfectly. It really is incredible!

Now let's get down to serious business. Even if you're not convinced that science is great and amazing and fun, the fact is you've got to learn it anyway, so you may as well be as good at it as you can. That's what this book is for—to help you do better in science. So let's get started!

Chapter 2
Your Science Book Is Your Friend

Do you and your science textbook have a good relationship? Did you know your science textbook can be a big help to you, especially if you know how to make the best use of it? The tips in this chapter can show you ways to make that big, heavy book worth the effort of lugging it to and from school every day!

1. *Take good care of your book!* Remember, your science book is your friend, so treat it nicely! Don't use it as a placemat for food or as second base in a softball game. It's meant to be *read.* Someday you may need to look at that chart or graph or explanation that got torn out or stained. This sounds simple, but it's important. You will need the book all through the school year, and it's easier to read and use for studying when it is clean. Also, though it's your book this year, other students will use it in the future, and they deserve to get a book in good condition.

2. *Read your assignment through.* When you are assigned pages to read in your textbook, read them straight through from beginning to end fairly quickly. Don't stop unless you come to sections that are hard to understand. Then stop only to make a note of those parts, and keep reading until you have finished the whole assignment. This is called *getting an overview* of the subject. Once you have read it through, if you understand the whole thing, you won't need to bother with the next tip.

3. *Read the hard parts again.* If there were sections of your assignment that you did not completely understand in your first read-through, go back and read those parts more slowly. You may get a clearer idea of what they are about just by taking your time and paying very close attention. If you find that you now understand the difficult parts better, read through the whole assignment one last time, so you can add them to your overview of the subject.

However, if you *still* don't get some parts, be sure to follow the next tip.

4. *Don't give up!* If you still don't understand that particularly tricky section of your assignment, just forgetting about it will not help you in the long run. Chances are you'll come to another section that you can't quite get unless you've managed to understand this one. Don't panic. Here are a few suggestions for what you can do next.

5. *Go to the library.* Sometimes going to the library is a pain, but it's usually worth it. At the library you can find lots of books to help you. The first place to look is in an encyclopedia. Look for the simplest one you can find. If you need still more information, use the card file or computer to locate your subject. Ask the librarian to help you, too. Most librarians love to help people find stuff. That's why they became librarians in the first place. Here's one more library tip that can be your "secret science weapon"—look for books that were written for younger readers. These books sometimes explain difficult concepts really well. (At the end of this book, you will find a helpful list of science books that includes several for younger readers.)

6. *Ask a friend or someone at home.* This is a good idea, especially if you know someone who is really strong in science. (And it's less of a pain than going to the library.) If a friend, classmate, or relative is trying to explain a concept to you and you still don't understand, ask the person to give you *concrete examples.* A concrete example relates to something you already know or have experienced.

7. *Ask a teacher.* Your teacher, or possibly another teacher, will be able to explain the text so it's clear to you. Remember, ask for examples if necessary.

8. *Read your assignment again.* Once you have worked out the meaning of the difficult sections of an assignment, read through the whole thing again so that you can put what you have learned into your overview.

9. *Take notes as you read.* A later chapter in this book explains how to take notes. You will find that making notes about what you have read in the textbook will help you in two important ways:

1. Writing down a brief summary of what you read helps you keep the lesson more clearly in your memory.

2. When you need to look back at earlier lessons, either while studying for a test or while refreshing your memory when doing other assignments, you'll find that going through notes or an outline takes less time than reading chapters from the textbook all over again.

To decide how to organize the notes you take from your textbook reading, look through the chapter on note taking and see which form is best for the assignment you are working on.

10. *Copy the labeled illustrations.* When there is a picture with labels—of a flower, or an atom, or the insides of an insect—make a sketch of the illustration in your notes, and include the labels. It doesn't matter if you're not a fabulous artist. Drawing the picture and writing in the labels is a good way to remember what you have learned, and it will also come in handy when you study for tests.

11. *Use the back of your textbook.* In the back of your textbook you will find two helpful sections. One is the *glossary,* which is like a brief dictionary that gives definitions of words you might not know. The other section is the *index.* This is an alphabetized list of subjects covered in the book, together with the page numbers on which you will find the subjects. For instance, if you don't remember where to find an explanation of a habitat, look up "habitat" in the index and you will find the page number you need.

12. *Make word lists.* Studying science means learning a lot of new words. At the end of your notes for each textbook assignment, jot down a list of new words you learned, along with their definitions.

13. *Do extra reading.* No, you're not having a bad dream. You did read those words: "Do extra reading." If you really want to be a science champ, go to the library and read more on the assigned subject. The students who do extra work are almost always the ones who really stand out. Maybe that's not your goal, but if it is, extra reading is one of the sure ways to help you achieve it.

14. *Do the optional activities.* Textbooks often suggest optional activities that students may want to try. When the book recommends additional activities, do them. They were put there to help you get a better understanding of the topic about which you are learning. Plus, doing the optional activities shows your teacher that you are taking an interest in the subject and that you are trying your absolute best.

Chapter 3

Notes Aren't Just for Music

Imagine that you are studying for a big test you have to take the next morning. Where do you start? You've got your homework assignments from the last three weeks, but they don't cover everything that will be on the test. And you've got your textbook. You could read over all the pages that the test will cover, but you'd probably still be reading at four o'clock in the morning and then fall asleep in the middle of the test.

But maybe you did what the top science students do because they know it is the best way to prepare for tests. You took notes, both on your reading assignments and on what your teacher said in class. Now you can read over your own neat, well-organized notes that nicely summarize everything you learned. You'll look back at the textbook when necessary, but you won't have to read whole sections over from beginning to end. Doesn't that sound great? Here's how to do it.

15. *Be prepared.* When you take notes as you read your homework assignment, and your pen runs out of ink or your pencil point breaks, you can simply stop reading and put your book down until you have sharpened your pencil or gotten a new pen and are ready to write again. If it happens while your teacher is explaining the human digestive system, you can't expect the lesson to stop while you run to the pencil sharpener or borrow another pen. So *be prepared* when you come to class. Always carry extra pens or pencils as part of your day-to-day school supplies. And be ready to learn as soon as you take your seat.

16. *Don't try to write down every word.* When you're taking notes in class, don't try to write down every word your teacher says. Your hand will get sore, and you won't be able to keep up anyway. You might end up trying so hard to write every word that you barely hear what your teacher is saying.

The first rule for taking good notes is to listen carefully and try to understand the concept your teacher is explaining. Listen for what you think may be *key ideas* or *explanations,* and write those down. Oh, and one more thing. Don't write whole sentences. You only need to jot down a few words that will remind you of that important concept. You can fill in additional information when you review your notes later in the day.

17. *Ask questions.* If you don't understand something your teacher says in class, ask for an explanation. It doesn't mean you're dumb, and your teacher won't mind. As a matter of fact, most teachers love it when kids ask questions. It means they're listening and they're interested. And they're probably doing some of the other kids a favor. Lots of students may have the same question, but few bother to raise their hands. If you still have trouble understanding your teacher's explanation, jot down the concept and ask for extra help after class.

18. *Keep your notes together.* A notebook is the best place to keep notes. That's why it's called a notebook. Scraps of paper, old envelopes, or blank index cards that happen to be lying around are *bad* places to keep notes, because they have a way of disappearing, being thrown out by accident, or getting eaten by the dog. The little piece of brown paper bag on which you are *certain* you jotted down the names of the different kinds of igneous rocks may disappear forever the night before your big earth-science test. So keep your notes neatly organized in a notebook. If you choose to use a loose-leaf binder for all subjects, make sure you use dividers so you can quickly locate your notes for each subject.

19. *Organize your notes.* Just as important as keeping your notes in one place is keeping them arranged in a logical way that makes them easy to understand. For example, if you've followed our advice, you've been taking notes on your textbook assignments. You've also been taking notes on the key ideas your teacher has mentioned in class. Spend a few extra moments each time you do a science homework assignment to add your class notes to your textbook notes. You will help yourself in two ways: you'll have all the facts about each topic in one place so that you won't accidentally skip over any; and you'll save time by not going through the same facts twice. Also, organizing your notes helps you to understand and remember the key ideas.

20. *Make outlines.* A great way to review your notes quickly is to make an outline. You're almost sure to find that just making the outline is a good way to organize and remember information.

To write a *formal outline,* you need to know the rules. First, identify main topics with Roman numerals. Under each main topic, label *subtopics* with indented capital letters. Subtopics can be divided into smaller subtopics, labeled with Arabic numerals that are further indented; still smaller subtopics get lowercase letters. Here's how part of a formal outline could be set up:

I. How plants are different from animals
   A. Plants can't move around
   B. Plants make their own food
II. What plants need
   A. Sunlight
   B. Water
   C. Carbon dioxide
III. What we get from plants
   A. Food
      1. Food from roots
         a. beets
         b. carrots
      2. Food from stems
         a. celery
         b. rhubarb
      3. Food from leaves
         a. lettuce
         b. spinach

21. *Use graphic organizers.* A formal outline may not always be the best way to arrange your notes. For example, if you are describing a process, such as how an insect develops from egg to adult, you might want to use a *flow chart*. But to show the body parts of an insect you would probably draw a *diagram* with labels. Sometimes you can simply make a *list*. A list would be an ideal reminder of the names of the different kinds of animal habitats—desert, forest, wetland, and so on. Just remember that the important thing is to arrange your information in a way that makes it as easy as possible to review, remember, and understand.

22. *Use Venn diagrams.* A Venn diagram can be such a useful study tool that it gets a tip all to itself. This kind of graphic organizer is great for comparing and contrasting two things or ideas. (Comparing means showing similarities; contrasting means showing differences.) For example, to show the similarities and differences between plants and animals, draw two overlapping circles, as on the next page. Label one circle Plants and the other Animals. Label the area where the circles overlap each other Both. In the Plant area, write the characteristics that *only* plants have; in the Animal area, write the characteristics that *only* animals have. In the Both area, write the characteristics that both plants and animals have. The Venn diagram on the next page shows you how it works.

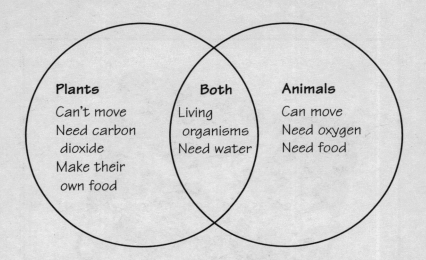

Plants
Can't move
Need carbon
  dioxide
Make their
  own food

Both
Living
  organisms
Need water

Animals
Can move
Need oxygen
Need food

23. *Make flash cards.* Flash cards can be a useful study aid, especially when you work with a partner. Let's say you need to study the parts of a flower. Start with a pile of index cards. On one side of each card, write the name of a flower part: petal, stamen, pistil, and so on. On the other side of each card, write the name of the part you noted on the front and a brief explanation of what that part does. You and a study partner can use the cards to take turns testing each other on the subject.

Chapter 4

The Test Is Tomorrow!

Just like your other teachers, once in a while your science teacher is bound to say these words: "There will be a test tomorrow." When that happens, stay calm. This doesn't have to be a disaster—especially if you start *now*, before your teacher even mentions that test, to work on developing *good study habits*. Heard that before? Well, just in case you are not sure exactly what those wonderful habits are, read this chapter. It can help you be a star at studying for a science test.

24. *Clean up your room.* Believe it or not, it helps. First of all, little items like notes and homework can get lost for days under a pile of CDs or comic books. But even more importantly, most people work and study better in a room that is clean and orderly. That doesn't mean you have to be a neat freak, but when there are heaps of clothes, games, or other stuff lying around, it is more difficult to concentrate on studying. Try it and see!

25. *Study regularly.* Don't wait until the day before a test to try to cram everything into your brain. Imagine what would happen if you didn't eat for a week and then tried to stuff a week's worth of breakfasts, lunches, and dinners into your stomach at one sitting. You'd probably get really sick, but let's not discuss the details. Let's just say that your brain, too, works better if you give it a little information each day. Make a habit of scheduling a certain amount of science time on most or all school days. It takes only a few minutes to read over your notes or skim your textbook, and those few minutes a day will help make studying for a test a breeze.

26. *Know what's best for you.* Some people study best with a partner; others just can't concentrate unless they're alone. Some students find background music relaxing, while others find it distracting. Think about how you study best, then make sure your study area has everything you need to do your best.

27. *Studying with partners can work—some of the time.* Two heads are sometimes better than one. When you use flash cards, for example, you'll need someone else to work with. Having a study partner can also be useful when you're trying to understand something really difficult. One of you might have a clearer grasp of the subject and be able to explain it to the other. Or you may be able to solve a problem when you exchange ideas with someone else. The important thing to remember is that studying with a partner will *not* work unless you keep in mind that you're together to study—not to watch TV or gab. Find a quiet place and get to work!

28. *Don't allow interruptions.* Schedule blocks of science study time for yourself. During that time, don't make or take phone calls or let anything unimportant stop your work. Can you imagine telling your parents not to call you to the phone during your study time? It might be worth it just to see the looks on their faces! (Don't worry, they may be surprised, but they won't faint.)

You may have to try several ways of studying to discover which works best for you. Some people find they can't absorb much information after fifteen minutes of studying. These people work best when they study for about fifteen minutes then take a short five-minute break. Others need to study for thirty minutes or more without interruptions to understand difficult concepts. Experiment with both methods. If you don't feel you are getting the best results with either regimen, talk to a teacher or counselor to find out how to maximize your study efforts.

29. *Make a note of the most difficult material.* Most students find certain science ideas particularly difficult to understand or remember. When you come across such an idea, don't get stuck on it. Write it down so you can come back to it. Or you might put a sticky note on the page in your textbook or notes. Then, you'll be able to return to that section to go over the concept until it becomes clearer and more fixed in your mind. If you simply cannot grasp the concept, ask a friend or your teacher to explain it to you.

30. *Refresh your memory on earlier work.* It's a good idea to start your science study sessions by reviewing some of the concepts you have studied already—especially the parts that you noted down as being unusually hard to learn. Once you have spent a little time going through this material, then you can turn your attention to new areas. That way everything will stay fresh in your memory.

31. *Let ROY G. BIV help your memory.* Have you ever heard of ROY G. BIV? He's not a famous scientist—in fact, he doesn't really exist. But ROY has been helping students remember the colors of the visible spectrum for many years. They are: Red, Orange, Yellow, Green, Blue, Indigo, and Violet. Put their first letters together, and you have ROY G. BIV. Memory helpers like this are called *mnemonics* (nee-MON-iks). You can make up your own mnemonics to help you remember facts that give you trouble. For example, if you need to remember the names of all the Great Lakes, think of the word HOMES—Huron, Ontario, Michigan, Erie, and Superior.

32. *Help your memory with word associations.* Here's another handy way to remember some of what you study. A scientific term may suggest an image, or another word, that helps you remember what that term means. For instance, *zoology* is the study of animals. Where can you find lots of animals? In the *zoo,* of course.

33. *Make sketches from textbook illustrations.* Sometimes you will need to study labeled textbook illustrations and to remember the names on the labels. Perhaps you'll have to learn the parts of a plant cell or the human digestive tract. To help yourself remember, try drawing a rough sketch of the illustration with the labels left blank. See if you can fill in the labels without looking at the book. If you can't get them all, try it again. After a few tries, you'll probably know them all. Ask a friend or parent to check your work.

34. *Sometimes you just have to memorize.* Sorry, but now and then you may not be able to find special tricks to help you keep facts and information in your head. When that happens, you may simply have to grit your teeth and go over that material . . . again and again, if necessary. This might not be a lot of fun, but it's an almost foolproof method. Review tip #26 to find out how you study best. Then take your textbook, your notes, and any other materials you may need and start memorizing!

35. *Test your understanding by teaching someone else.* As you prepare for a test, you can see how thorough your grasp of a science topic is by becoming a teacher for a little while. Explain what you've been studying to a volunteer "student"—maybe a brother, sister, parent, or friend. If this other person can follow your explanations, then you probably have a good understanding of the subject.

Chapter 5

The Right Way to Do a Science Experiment

Here's a true story about a science experiment. The student's name has been changed.

Laura likes music. She plays it all the time. She also likes to grow plants, and she's known for having a green thumb. One day Laura gets a hunch that the reason her plants are so healthy is because she keeps them in the same room with the stereo. When Laura's teacher says everyone has to do an independent science project, Laura decides to do an experiment to find out if she is right about her plants.

She plants some seeds and puts half the baby plants near the window in the room with the stereo. She puts the rest of the plants in a dark closet where they can't "hear" the music. She waters all the plants at the same time. After several weeks, the "music plants" are big and healthy. The ones in the closet are dead. Laura concludes that she was right: music is good for growing plants.

Laura made one big mistake in her experiment. Can you figure out what she did wrong? As you read this chapter, ask yourself which tips would have helped Laura set up a more scientific experiment—and get a better grade.

36. *Learn to be a good observer.* The first step in being a good scientist or science student is to notice what goes on around you. You can actually practice and improve this skill.

Take a piece of paper and a pencil, and find a comfortable place to sit, outdoors or indoors. Spend ten or fifteen minutes looking at your surroundings and then jot down five things that impress you. They don't have to be things you see. They can also be sounds or smells or even sensations, such as hot and cold temperatures. As you work at developing your powers of observation, you will notice things that you never have before. Laura observed that her plants near the stereo and the window were growing unusually fast.

37. *Learn to ask "Why?"* After you make an observation, your next step as a scientist is to think about the causes of what you observe. Would you like to know why the bread baking in the kitchen can be smelled all over the house . . . or why some things float while others sink? Maybe you, like Laura, wonder if music is helping your plants grow.

38. *Make guesses.* If you decide to try to answer your own question by setting up a science experiment, stop right here. According to the process called the *scientific method,* you should *make a guess* before you think about your experiment. Don't make a wild guess, but an "educated guess." That means *use what you already know* to figure out a possible answer. To go back to the plant question, for example, you might guess that, because you play music all the time and your plants are particularly healthy, music helps plants grow. This kind of guess is called a *hypothesis.*

39. *Test your hypothesis.* Now that you have made an observation and come up with a hypothesis that might explain it, you're ready to set up your experiment in order to *test* your hypothesis. You plant some seeds in a flowerpot and leave the pot in a room with the stereo turned on. If the seeds grow, the experiment supports your hypothesis. Right? Wrong. What is wrong with this experiment?

40. *An experiment needs a control.* Laura did part of her experiment according to the scientific method. She knew that to find out whether plants respond to music, she would need not one, but *two* groups of plants—one group that would "hear" music, and one group that would not. The plants that Laura kept near the window in the room with the stereo are called the *test group;* the plants in the closet are the *control group.*

41. *An experiment must have only one variable.* Laura was doing pretty well. She made an observation, asked a question, made an educated guess about the answer (her hypothesis), set up a test, and made sure to use a control group. So what was wrong with her experiment? True, the plants in the closet didn't get to "hear" the music, but what else didn't they get? Sunlight! So how can we tell if the plants died from lack of music or lack of sunlight? The test-group plants were near a sunny window. The differences in the conditions for the test group and the control group are called *variables.* A good experiment has *only one variable;* Laura's experiment had two—music or no music, and sunlight or no sunlight. How would you get rid of the extra variable if you were conducting this experiment? Do you think the results of your experiment would be the same as Laura's or different?

42. *Repeat your experiment.* It is often a good idea to do your experiment more than once to make sure you get the same results. If your results differ greatly each time you do your experiment, make sure you are setting the experiment up exactly the same way each time. Then go through each step carefully.

43. *Draw a conclusion.* You've got the results of your experiment. In fact, you did your experiment three times and got the same results every time. Now you need to *interpret* those results. What do they mean? Your answer to that question is your *conclusion*. The conclusion should be brief, but it should also answer your question thoroughly. You can use charts, graphs, or illustrations to make your conclusion clearer.

44. *An experiment doesn't really prove anything!* Does this surprise you? If you are thinking like a scientist, you understand that the results of an experiment either support your hypothesis or they don't. Every experiment that does support your hypothesis makes a stronger case for it. But it's always possible that another experiment under different conditions could end up with different results—and a different conclusion.

45. *No experiment is a "failure."* What if your experiment doesn't support your hypothesis? Is it a failure? *No!* Whatever the results of your experiment, if you set it up correctly, with a control group and only one variable, you've learned something. Since learning more about the world around us is the whole point of science, your experiment has been a success!

46. *Be fair.* It's important to remember tip #45, because knowing that your experiment will be successful no matter how it turns out will keep you from setting up your experiment so that the test group will "win." If you're like most people, you will want your results to support your hypothesis—so maybe you will just forget to water the control plants a few times. Or perhaps you will give the test plants some plant food, but neglect to feed the control plants. That's not fair, because you're adding more variables and making your results less meaningful. You will learn the most from a tightly controlled, well-designed experiment.

47. *Practice drawing.* Oh, no! Now we're into art? No. Still on science. The point of science is to learn about your world, and part of learning is to share what you have discovered. That's why you'll want to write up a report describing your experiment and the results. Those who read your report will get much more out of it if you include pictures and diagrams that back up your words.

Some people are naturally good at drawing, but even if you're not one of them, you can improve your drawing skills with practice. Really. Try making drawings of household objects, like a telephone or clock. Take drawing materials outside and try making pictures of a tree, a flowering plant, a squirrel, or a bird. You may not turn out to be the next Rembrandt, but you'll be able to show, as well as tell, your readers what you did and what you found out.

48. *Take photos!* Do you want to make your reports really impressive? Take photos of each stage of your experiment! Photos will help people reading your report visualize each phase. The facts will be clearer, and you won't have to draw pictures. Just remember to leave time to get your photos developed!

Chapter 6
Science, Writing, and You

Writing? Wait a minute! Don't you learn about writing in language arts class? Do scientists use a different language? Do they have their own special grammar rules? Are you going to have to learn how to write *all over again*?

No, you won't. Everything you've learned in language arts also applies to science writing. But certain things are especially important when you write a science report or describe a science project. Knowing these tips can make your report or project a real success.

49. *Introduce your subject.* Begin your science reports, like all your compositions, with an introduction. Explain the topic about which you'll be writing, and describe the observations that suggested your project or experiment. Laura, for example, liked playing music for her plants, so she might have begun her report by writing, "I have always loved music. I am also good at growing plants. I started wondering if there was a connection between the fact that I have music playing in my room all the time and the fact that the plants in my room seem particularly healthy."

50. *State your hypothesis. Hypothesis* is a fancy word for an educated guess about what the result of an experiment will be, based on the information you already have. (If you need to refresh your memory, go back to Chapter 5.) Follow your introduction with a clear statement of your hypothesis. Laura's hypothesis could have been stated like this: "Plants grow better when they are in a room where music is being played."

51.

Write a complete list of materials. Your report should be so clear and complete that a person reading it would be able to repeat your experiment step by step. This means that you need to give readers a complete list of everything you used to do your experiment. List your materials in the same order in which you used them.

EQUIPMENT LIST

- 1 PACK SEEDS
- POTTING SOIL
- FOUR 3-INCH POTS
- WATER
- SUNLIGHT

52. *Write the body of your report.* The main part of your report will be a step-by-step description of everything you did for your experiment or project, and exactly how you did each step. Before you begin writing, make an outline of all the steps needed to complete your experiment. Follow the outline when writing, filling in additional information if necessary. Try to be as concise as possible—long, rambling sentences will only bore and confuse the reader. State your findings as clearly as possible.

53. *Use the format your teacher prefers.* Your teacher might want you to write your report in paragraphs, like any other report, or in the form of a numbered list, with a number for each step and its details. If you're not sure, check with your teacher. If your teacher doesn't have a preference, use the format you're most comfortable with.

54. *Use chronological order. Chronological order* is another one of those fancy phrases. This one means "time order." Describe things in the order in which you did them, and describe your results in the order in which they occurred.

55. *Use formal language.* Formal language doesn't require big words. It simply means that your report should read more as though you were giving a speech than as though you were talking to a friend on the phone. Be sure to use correct grammar and spelling, and—unlike this book—avoid contractions. Write "did not" instead of "didn't," "will not" instead of "won't," and so on. Have a dictionary and thesaurus handy in case you need to look words up.

56. *Use precise language.* Science requires you to be precise. For example, if you give plants one ounce (or 25 ml) of water every day, write down the exact amount. It's not enough simply to say that you gave the plants "some water."

57. *Stick to the facts.* Science deals with *facts*. You should limit yourself to facts and stay away from expressing opinions. For example, if you do an experiment in which some plants live and others die, the fact that some plants lived and stayed healthy is not *good;* it just *is*. Neither is the fact that other plants withered and died *too bad* or *unfortunate*. These are words that express opinions, not facts.

58. *Use diagrams, graphs, and charts.* When you use

these visual aids, you do two things: you make your report more interesting and varied to look at, and you provide readers with a vivid and helpful way to understand what you did. Laura, for example, might have improved her report by making a graph like the one below to show how much the test plants grew during a given time period.

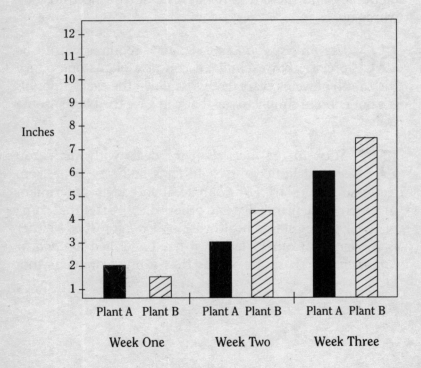

59. *Summarize your results.* After you have described your experiment, the next step is to write a simple and straightforward summary of the results. Laura's summary might have been: "Plants grew more quickly when they were in a room where music was played."

60. *Interpret your results.* Tell what you think your results mean based on what you know from the experiment you performed. Here's what Laura could have written: "I interpret these results to mean that music has a positive effect on the growth of plants." Another expression for interpreting results is *drawing a conclusion.*

61. *Suggest practical uses for your results, if you can think of any.* If you believe that the results of your experiment have a practical use, let your readers know. Laura might have written, "If farmers had stereo speakers in their fields, they might find an increase in their crops."

62. *List any research sources you used.* You may or may not have needed to do research for your project. If you did, prepare a bibliography that includes all your sources of information. Give the name of the author or authors—last name first, followed by a period—and then the title, which you should underline, as in this example:

Green, Greta. <u>Fun with Plants.</u>

Check with your teacher to find out if he or she wants you to do a more detailed bibliography, including the name of the publisher and place and date the book was published. If so, use the bibliography at the back of this book as a guide for setting yours up. If you used more than one book, list the titles alphabetically by authors' last names. If an author wrote more than one book in your bibliography, follow the style used in the bibliography at the back of this book.

63. *Reread your report and look for errors—carefully!* Once you have written a rough draft of your report, you should reread it very carefully to make sure that all of it is correct. Is your list of materials complete? Did you list the items in the proper order? Did you accidentally leave out any steps in the experiment? Correct any mistakes you find. The answer to the question "How do you proofread a science report?" is "Very carefully."

64. *Proofread for style.* Especially in science, it's important to write clearly—and that usually means using simple language. Look through your draft to see if you can find long, complicated sentences that might confuse readers. If you see some, break them down into shorter, simpler sentences. Here's an example.

Too long and complex:

The plants that were put on the window ledge where they were able to get a lot of sun grew large and healthy, while the other plants that had been left in a dark room in which there was little or no sunlight began to wither after a day or so and finally died after approximately a week.

Better:

The plants on the sunny window ledge grew large and healthy. The ones in the dark room began to wither after two days. By the end of the week they had died.

One good way to be sure that your report is clear and understandable is to give it to a classmate or parent to read through. Ask your proofreader to point out anything that needs to be clarified. You might offer to do the same thing for your classmate.

Chapter 7

Come to the Fair . . . the Science Fair!

Does your school have a science fair every year? Does your teacher ask you to do a special science project? Don't worry. This chapter gives you tips on how to plan and complete a science project you can be proud of.

65. *Don't put it off!* Usually you'll have plenty of time to create a science project. But don't be fooled into thinking that you can put this assignment aside until the last week or so. If you want to do it right, start to work on the project as soon as possible—and that means *now.* You need to come up with a topic, do research, create an experiment, and allow enough time to complete your experiment.

66. *Choose a subject that interests you.* Chances are that some science topics interest you more than others. Like Laura, you may think plants are fascinating. Maybe you're more interested in animals than plants, or perhaps you like rocks more than either plants or animals. If you are especially interested in any particular branch of science, then that's the area for you to concentrate on when you begin developing a project.

67. *Choose a practical topic.* What does "practical" mean? First of all, it means that you shouldn't try to tackle a subject that would be impossible to experiment with. For instance, you won't be able to work with a nuclear reactor, so it's a bad idea to choose a project that requires nuclear energy—although a solar-energy project would probably be fine. Stay away from anything that could be dangerous. A project on rattlesnakes, for instance, is a bad idea, but you could come up with a good project using earthworms. And you should consider the area in which you live when you choose your project. If you live in the desert, for example, a project involving the ocean or tide pools probably wouldn't be best. How would you conduct experiments and gather data if you don't live near the ocean? Stick with a subject about which you have some basic knowledge.

68. *Try for an original idea.* Spend a little time and see if you can come up with a subject that is unusual enough to get people's attention. Lots of kids do projects to show that plants need sunlight, for example, but how many try to see whether plants grow better with *music*? Think of your poor teacher and whoever else will judge your project. They have to look at project, after project, after—well, you get the idea. Give them an original topic that they haven't already seen forty-seven times, and they'll enjoy your presentation more. They might even reward you with a better grade, too.

69. *Get help finding an idea.* If you are having trouble coming up with an idea, here are a few ways to get help. You might talk to a teacher or to a parent. If you or your family knows anyone who is professionally connected with science in some way, you could ask that person to help you develop a project idea. And, of course, there are loads of ideas in the books at your school or local library. You can probably even find a book of science-project ideas. Finally, don't underestimate your friends. Sometimes just talking something over with a classmate can help you get ideas.

70. *Don't make your topic too general.* "What makes plants grow?" is *not* a good question to begin with. It's too general. Remember that you'll have to offer a possible answer as your hypothesis, and there's just no way to state a reasonable hypothesis for such a big question. Narrow your topic down to something more precise. *The effect of music on plants.* Now there's a topic for you!

71. *Do research.* When you work on a science project, you will probably need a more thorough knowledge of your subject than your textbook can give you. That means you'll need to do some *research* in the library. Don't be scared by the idea of doing research. You'll find that libraries are not hard to use. Many of them now have computer terminals where you can type in your subject and get a list of books to read. If you need help getting started, remember that's what librarians are there for. Don't be afraid to ask for their help. One more thing about research. As you read and take notes, be sure to copy down the author and title of each book you use so that you can find the book again if you have to. You'll also need this information for the bibliography at the end of your report.

72. *Gather everything you need.* Before you start working on your project, make a list of every single thing you will need and get those things together. Otherwise, you might be caught right in the middle of your project without the equipment or materials you need to complete it.

73. *Once you've started, don't neglect your experiment.* Most experiments will need your attention for at least a few minutes each day. For example, if you were Laura you'd want to decide how many times a week your plants need to be watered. Write down your watering schedule, and then stick to it. Your neatly written schedule would make a nice addition to your project report.

74. *Keep a log.* No, not a piece of wood. We mean the kind of log that is like a diary. For an experiment like Laura's, you'd want to check both sets of plants each day, make notes about whatever you observed, and draw pictures showing what the plants from each group looked like each day. And you'd want to write the date and time you took each set of notes. Remember that science reports are supposed to contain exact information, so you'll be very glad to have your observations, notes, and pictures—along with dates and times—when it comes time to write your report.

75. *Write your report.* Once you complete your experiment, it will be time to write it up as a report. Check with your teacher for the proper format—can the report be handwritten, or should it be typed? How many pages should it be? Your report should follow this basic outline:

- title page
- table of contents (Many people find it helpful to do this last. Others like to use their table of contents as a mini-outline for all the things they need to include in their report. Either way, wait until you finish your report before plugging in the page numbers.)
- introduction explaining why you chose your topic and giving readers any special information they will need to understand it
- hypothesis
- list of materials you used, in the order you used them
- step-by-step description of how you set up your project and tested your hypothesis (including pictures, photos, diagrams, and charts)
- results, or how your experiment turned out
- conclusion, or what you think your results mean
- bibliography listing any books you used for your project

Follow the tips in Chapter 6 as you work.

76. Know the rules.

If you've been to science fairs before, you may have noticed that most projects were designed in a similar way. That's because there are special rules each student must follow when preparing a science experiment. The list below presents some general rules most science fairs follow. Check with your teacher to see if your school has other rules for science fairs.

- Each student may have only one project.
- Projects must follow the scientific method (see Chapter 5).
- Students must make sure their projects are safe and will not harm anyone.
- Students must be available to answer questions from the judges during fair hours.
- The maximum exhibit size is usually 4 feet (1.2 m) wide x 2 ½ feet (0.76 m) deep x 6 ½ feet (1.9 m) tall.

77. *Make your display.* Now that you know what size your display should be, here's how to set it up:

- Use three panels of stiff cardboard, foamboard, or other sturdy material. Fasten the panels so that they stand up by themselves, as in the picture below.

- The center panel usually contains the title page and table of contents, along with an illustration (or two) of your project. These can be drawn by hand or on the computer—or you may wish to use photographs.

- The panel on the left usually includes the introduction, a list of materials, and your hypothesis.

- The panel on the right includes your step-by-step description of the project, your results, and your conclusion.

- On the table in front of your three-part display you should place an actual part of your experiment (for example, a plant that lived and a plant that died). Label all parts of your experiment.

- Make your display as interesting as possible. Include charts and graphs and any other material that will make your project stand out.

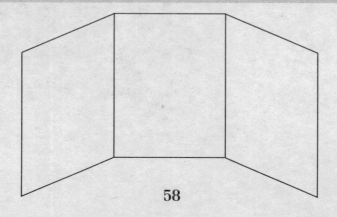

78.

Prepare an oral report. If you will be giving an oral report about your project, you'd better prepare for it. Different ways of preparing work best for different people, so choose the one that's best for you. Here are several techniques to consider:

- Write out what you will say, memorize it, and then recite it from memory. Remember to be expressive as you speak, so you won't sound like you're reciting from memory, even though everyone knows you are. You might want to jot down notes of your most important points on index cards. Keep the cards with you when you give your report, just in case you forget something. Knowing you have this information on hand will also give you more confidence.

- Write out your whole speech and read it aloud. This is the safest way, but you run the risk of sounding boring, especially if you never make eye contact with your listeners. Try to look up at your audience as many times as possible during your presentation. And read with expression, as if you were just talking to a close friend.

Whichever method you choose, practice your oral report a few times before you give it in public. You can use your friends or family as a practice audience. If you have a time limit, ask someone to time you to make sure you're not running too long.

Most students are a little nervous about giving oral reports, so it would be silly to say "Don't be nervous." However, you can be sure that if you've prepared and practiced, you'll be much less nervous than you would be otherwise.

79. *Answer, please.* Some of the people who see your display may have questions. After completing the experiment and writing your report, you should be able to answer any question! If there are some facts you're afraid you may forget, jot them down on index cards. Keep the cards in your pocket or behind the display for quick reference.

Chapter 8
Helpful Odds and Ends

Here are some other tips and useful pieces of information that might come in handy during your science studies.

80. *Learn the metric system.* In most countries of the world, measurements are not made in inches, feet, and miles, ounces and pounds, or quarts and gallons. Instead, the metric system of measurements is used. It is also the standard system used by scientists all over the world, including those living in the United States. The other system, which may be more familiar to you, is usually called the English system, since most of the measurement units it uses were originally developed in England.

Once you learn how the metric system works—and it's easy to learn—you'll see why many people prefer it. The English system uses many different units to measure with, and they can be difficult to convert from one to another. For example, one foot equals twelve inches, and 5,280 feet equal one mile. How many inches are there in three quarters of a mile? It's not that easy to figure out! Or try this: one pound equals sixteen ounces, and one ton equals two thousand pounds. How many ounces are there in 2.74 tons?

In contrast, the metric system uses one basic unit for each kind of measurement. The unit of weight is the *gram*. The unit of length is the *meter*. The unit of volume is the *liter*. That's all. For larger or smaller figures, you just add *prefixes* to these units. One of these prefixes is *kilo*, meaning "one thousand." One thousand meters equals one *kilometer*. Can you guess another way to say "one thousand grams"?

If you said, "one kilogram," you've almost mastered the metric system! It's much easier to figure out how many grams there are in 1.75 kilograms than it would be to work out the number of ounces in 1.75 pounds. Here is a table of prefixes used in the metric system:

mega-	equals	one million (1,000,000)
kilo-	equals	one thousand (1,000)
hecto-	equals	one hundred (100)
deka-	equals	ten (10)
deci-	equals	one tenth (.1)
centi-	equals	one hundredth (.01)
milli-	equals	one thousandth (.001)
micro-	equals	one millionth (.000001)

A *micrometer* equals one millionth of a meter. A *hectogram* is one hundred grams. What would you call ten liters? What would you call one hundredth of a meter?

If your answers are a *dekaliter* and a *centimeter,* then you have just passed this test of the metric system with an A+! Ask your teacher which measuring system you should use in your writing and projects. You may even want to write down both, putting one in parentheses, like these examples:

70.74 inches (1.8 meters)
18.7 ounces (551.6 milliters)
7 pounds (3,178 grams)

On the following pages, you'll find a table of information about the English measurement system and *conversion tables* that will help you work out what something measured with a metric unit is equal to when measured with the English system and *vice versa.*

THE ENGLISH MEASUREMENT SYSTEM

Length
	Equals
One foot (ft.)	12 inches (in.)
One yard (yd.)	3 feet
One mile (mi.)	5,280 feet or 1,760 yards

Weight
	Equals
One pound (lb.)	16 ounces (oz.)
One ton	2,000 pounds

Volume
	Equals
One cup (c.)	8 ounces (oz.)
One pint (pt.)	2 cups
One quart (qt.)	2 pints
One gallon (gal.)	4 quarts

CONVERTING ENGLISH TO
METRIC MEASUREMENTS

Length
Equals

One inch (in.)	2.54 centimeters (cm)
One foot (ft.)	30.48 centimeters
One mile (mi.)	1.6 kilometers (km)

Weight
Equals

One ounce (oz.)	28.4 grams (g)
One pound (lb.)	454 grams
One ton	908 kilograms (kg)

Volume
Equals

One ounce (oz.)	29.5 milliliters (ml)
One pint (pt.)	473 milliliters
One quart (qt.)	946 milliliters
One gallon (gal.)	3.79 liters (l)

CONVERTING METRIC TO ENGLISH MEASUREMENTS

Length
Equals

One centimeter (cm)	0.39 inch (in.)
One meter (m)	39.3 inches, 3.28 feet (ft.), or 1.09 yards (yd.)
One kilometer (km)	0.62 miles (mi.)

Weight
Equals

One gram (g)	0.035 ounce (oz.)
One kilogram (kg)	2.2 pounds (lb.)

Volume
Equals

One liter (l)	1.06 quarts (qt.)
One centiliter (cl)	.176 ounce (oz.)

81.

There are two ways to measure temperature! What is the temperature at which water freezes? Is it 32° or is it 0°? Whichever answer you gave, you were right!

That's because, just as there are two ways to measure length, weight, and volume, there are also two ways to measure temperature. The *Fahrenheit* scale gives 32° as the temperature at which water freezes. (By the way, the symbol ° stands for "degrees.") But the freezing temperature of water is 0° according to the *Celsius* scale. Water boils at 212° Fahrenheit—or 212°F. It boils at 100° Celsius, or 100°C. Check with your teacher to find out which temperature scale you should use in your science writing and work, and be sure to use the appropriate abbreviation—*F* or *C*—when writing temperatures, so that there will not be any confusion about which system you are working with.

To convert Fahrenheit into Celsius, follow these steps:

1. From the number of degrees Fahrenheit that you want to convert into Celsius, first subtract 32.

2. Multiply the result by 5.

3. Divide that figure by 9 . . . and you have the equivalent measurement in degrees Celsius.

For instance, the boiling point of water is 212°F. Subtract 32, and you get 180. Then, 180 x 5 equals 900. Divide 900 by 9, and you get 100. And 100° is the boiling point of water in the Celsius system.

To convert Celsius into Fahrenheit, follow these steps:

> 1. Divide the number of degrees Celsius you want to convert by 5.
>
> 2. Multiply the resulting number by 9.
>
> 3. Add 32 to that result, and you have the Fahrenheit reading that equals your Celsius reading.

Let's say you want to convert 36°C into Fahrenheit. Divide 36 by 5, and you get 7.2. Multiply 7.2 by 9, and the answer is 64.8. Add 32, and the result is 96.8, which you can then round out to 97. So 36°C equals roughly 97°F.

82. *Keep clean!* When scientists are at work in a laboratory or workshop, they keep things orderly. Labs are *never* allowed to get dirty because dirt can damage delicate equipment and distort the results of scientific work. When you work on experiments and projects, do what real scientists do and keep things clean and tidy.

Whether you're working in a kitchen, your room, or someplace else, be sure that the floor is protected against spills and stains by spreading newspaper on it. Cover tables or other work surfaces with newspapers too.

Be sure that you know where everything you need for your project can be found. Studying is easier and more effective in a neat room, and the same thing is true of doing experiments. If you need a measuring cup *right now,* it's no fun to have to spend an hour hunting for it.

By the way, don't forget to include *yourself* among the things you'll want to keep clean. Scientists wear special laboratory clothing, and you'll probably want to do the same thing. You may not have lab coats around the house, but a smock or apron will keep your clothes from getting messed up.

83. *Safety first.* This may be the most important tip you'll read in this book:

Be careful!

Sometimes a project or experiment may call for the use of a knife or other sharp tool. In certain cases you may have to heat something on a stove.

Such tasks are best left in the hands of adults. Be sure that you ask for their help when using anything sharp or hot.

You may also need a grownup to give you a hand with some equipment. Don't hesitate to ask for help or advice from a parent, older relative, teacher, or other adult when you aren't sure how to use a piece of equipment, especially anything delicate or complicated.

Remember, safety is as important in your science studies as it is in everything else you do.

84. *Science, science everywhere!* There are many different branches of science, each focusing on a particular area. Here are just a few of them.

Anthropology—the study of human beings
Archaeology—the study of past human life
Astronomy—the study of heavenly bodies
Bacteriology—the study of bacteria
Biology—the study of life forms and living creatures
Botany—the study of plants
Chemistry—the study of elements and compounds
Cosmology—the study of the nature of the universe
Dendrology—the study of trees
Ecology—the study of environment
Entomology—the study of insects
Geology—earth science
Herpetology—the study of reptiles and amphibians
Ichthyology—the study of fish
Meteorology—the study of weather
Mineralogy—the study of minerals
Mycology—the study of mushrooms and other funguses
Oceanography—the study of oceans

Paleontology—the study of prehistoric life on earth

Physics—the study of matter and energy

Physiology—the study of body organs and systems

Psychology—the study of the mind and behavior

Sociology—the study of society

Zoology—the study of animal life

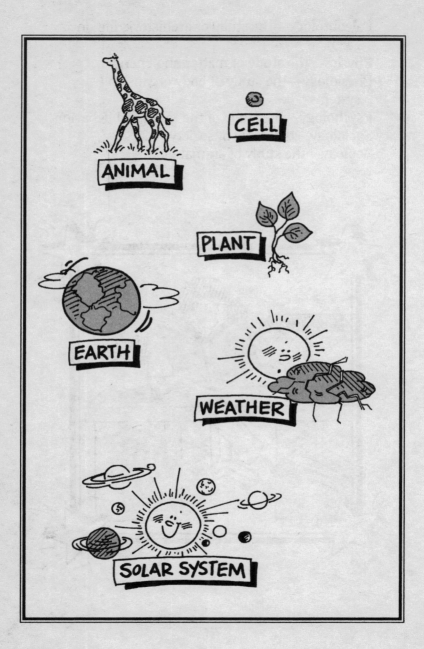

CELL

ANIMAL

PLANT

EARTH

WEATHER

SOLAR SYSTEM

Chapter 9

Science Terms You'll Be Glad You Know

Science is full of special words you don't normally use. For example, you don't usually go around saying such things as, "I went to a really great *ecosystem* over spring break," or "That balloon will pop if you blow in any more *carbon dioxide.*" That's why getting to know these terms will help you do better in science. When you read or hear them, you won't feel like you're trying to understand a foreign language.

There are so many special science terms, it would take many books to list them all. This chapter defines a few terms to help get you started. We cheated a little by including several terms within one definition. (The science terms are in **boldface** type, so you can find them easily. If you see a word in *italics,* that means it appears as a main term in another tip.)

85. **animal** A living organism that can move from place to place and eats *plants* or other animals. There are many different kinds of animals, including fish, birds, insects, and mammals. **Mammals** have fur or hair, do not lay eggs, and give milk to their babies. Humans, dogs, and cats are mammals.

86. **atmosphere** The air that surrounds Earth.

87. **biome** A habitat having a particular combination of *plants* and *animals*. There are six biomes. **Deserts** contain little plant life and have low rainfall; **grasslands** contain many grasses but few trees; **taigas** contain many cone-bearing trees; **deciduous forests** contain many leaf-bearing trees; **tundras** have little rainfall, and temperatures are cold; **tropical rain forests** have much rainfall, warm temperatures, and many green plants.

88. **cell** The smallest unit of living matter that can live independently.

89. **embryo** A living organism that is just beginning to develop.

90. **endangered species** A type of *plant* or *animal* that is in danger of becoming **extinct**, or being wiped out.

91. **food chain** The "eating path" from one living organism to another in a group. A food chain contains **producers** (living organisms that are eaten by others), **consumers** (living organisms that eat food provided by the producers), and **decomposers** (living organisms, such as bacteria, that break down the remains of dead organisms). Producers may be either *plants* or *animals*. There are three types of consumers: **carnivores** eat only other animals; **herbivores** eat only plants; **omnivores** eat both animals and plants. (For example, lions are carnivores, cows are herbivores, and human beings are omnivores.)

92. **galaxy** A huge group of stars, held together by gravity. **Gravity** is the force that pulls objects toward one another. For example, gravity keeps us from flying off Earth, and it holds the *solar system* together.

93. **matter** Any substance that takes up space. There are three kinds of matter. **Liquid,** such as water, can be poured and takes the shape of any container; **solid,** such as wood, has a shape of its own and has hardness; **gas,** such as oxygen, has no shape, cannot be poured, and is usually invisible.

94. **mineral** A solid, such as iron, that does not come from a living organism. **Rocks** are made of minerals. There are three kinds of rocks. **Igneous rocks** are formed from the melted rock that flows when a volcano erupts, then cools and hardens. **Sedimentary rocks** are formed from bits of rocks and minerals and pieces of dead plants or animals that harden in layers. **Metamorphic rocks** form from rocks that are changed by being heated or compressed.

95. **plant** A living organism that cannot move from place to place by itself and that makes its own food. The most important parts of a plant are **roots,** which grow toward water and bring water to rest of the plant; **stems,** which grow toward light and carry water to the leaves; and **leaves,** which use sunlight, carbon dioxide, and water to make food for the plant. **Photosynthesis** is the process by which a plant makes its own food, using sunlight, carbon dioxide, and water.

96. **reflection** The bouncing of light off a surface. You can see yourself in a mirror because light bounces off the mirror and back toward your eyes.

97. **satellite** A natural or human-built object that revolves around another object in space. For example, the moon is a satellite of Earth.

98. **senses** The means by which *animals* can experience the world around them. Our five senses are sight, hearing, touch, taste, and smell.

99. **solar system** Any star and the objects that revolve around it. For example, the sun and the planets and other objects that move around, or **orbit,** it make up a solar system.

100. **universe** Everything that exists.

101. water cycle   The process by which water moves between Earth's surface and the air around it. Precipitation—such as rain, snow, hail, and sleet—falls and collects as water in oceans, lakes, and rivers. Energy from the sun causes this water to **evaporate,** or go back into the atmosphere in the form of **water vapor.** When water vapor cools, it **condenses,** or turns into *liquid* water, then falls to Earth's surface once again as precipitation.

Appendix
Bibliography Cards

Get organized! From reading this book you know that you will need to include in your science report a list of all the books and magazines you use for research. Photocopy the cards below, cut them out, and use one for each reference source. You can find the date and place of publication on the copyright page at the front of a book. For a magazine article, list the date on the front cover of the magazine, but you do not need to include a place of publication.

If you do on-line research, list the name and address of the website you visited on the card. You may not have to include on-line research in your bibliography, but it's helpful to have the information in case you need to go back and confirm facts.

Bibliography Card

Title: _____

Author:_____

Publisher: _____

Place of Publication: _____

Date of Publication:_____

Pages Referred To: _____

Bibliography Card

Title: _____

Author: _____

Publisher: _____

Place of Publication: _____

Date of Publication: _____

Pages Referred To: _____

Bibliography Card

Title: _____

Author: _____

Publisher: _____

Place of Publication: _____

Date of Publication: _____

Pages Referred To: _____

Science Report Checklist

Make sure your reports are complete. Copy this list every time you do a science report. As you complete each step, either check it off or write in the date you finished. You'll feel great as you work through this list!

Report Checklist ✔

- ☐ Outline
- ☐ Introduction
- ☐ Hypothesis statement
- ☐ Materials list
- ☐ Body
- ☐ Results
- ☐ Practical uses for results
- ☐ Bibliography
- ☐ Proofread report
- ☐ Write neat, final copy

Bibliography

We've compiled a short list of great science books. Read through the list and choose a topic that interests you. Then go to your library and start reading! Your librarian can help you find more books on the topic you choose. Don't forget to check the back of each book for even more sources on your topic.

Alexander, Alison, and Susie Bower. *Science Magic: Scientific Experiments for Young Children*. New York: Simon & Schuster, 1986.

Allison, Linda. *The Reason for Seasons*. Boston: Little, Brown and Company, 1975.

Ardley, Neil. *The Science Book of Color*. New York: Harcourt Brace Jovanovich, 1991.

———. *The Science Book of Light*. New York: Harcourt Brace Jovanovich, 1991.

———. *Discovering Electricity*. New York: Simon & Schuster, 1992.

Berger, Gilda. *The Human Body*. New York: Doubleday, 1989.

Berger, Melvin. *Planets, Stars, and Galaxies*. New York: Putnam, 1977.

———. *Germs Make Me Sick!* New York: HarperCollins, 1995.

Booth, Jerry. *The Big Beast Book: Dinosaurs and How They Got That Way.* Boston: Little, Brown and Company, 1988.

Burns, Marilyn. *Good For Me! All About Food in 32 Bites.* Boston: Little, Brown, and Company, 1978.

Elting, Mary. *The Macmillan Book of Dinosaurs and Other Prehistoric Creatures.* New York: Macmillan, 1984.

Farndon, John. *How the Earth Works.* Pleasantville, NY: Reader's Digest Books, 1992.

Gaskin, John. *The Senses.* New York: Franklin Watts, 1985.

Haluch, Bill. *Magnetude.* Boston: Addison-Wesley Publishing Co., 1996.

Hann, Judith. *How Science Works.* Pleasantville, NY: Reader's Digest Books, 1991

Hirschfeld, Robert, and Nancy White. *The Kids' Science Book.* Charlotte, VT: Williamson Publishing, 1995.

Jobb, Jamie. *The Night Sky Book.* Boston: Little, Brown & Company, 1977.

Kettelkamp, Larry. *The Magic of Sound*. New York: Morrow, 1982.

Markle, Sandra. *The Young Scientist's Guide to Successful Science Projects*. New York: Beech Tree Books, 1990.

Milord, Susan. *The Kids' Nature Book*. Charlotte, VT: Williamson Publishing, 1989.

Smithsonian Family Learning Project. *The Science Activity Book*. New York: GMG Publishing, 1987.

Smolinski, Jill. *50 Nifty, Super Science Fair Projects*. Los Angeles: Lowell House, 1995.

Stein, Sara. *The Science Book*. New York: Workman Publishing, 1979.

Tucci, Salvatore. *How to Do a Science Fair Project*. New York: Franklin Watts, 1986.

Van Cleave, Janice Pratt. *Chemistry for Every Kid: 101 Easy Experiments That Really Work*. New York: John Wiley & Sons, 1989.

——. *Two Hundred & One Awesome, Magical, Bizarre, and Incredible Experiments*. New York: John Wiley & Sons, 1994.

Walpole, Brenda. *175 Science Experiments to Amuse and Amaze Your Friends*. New York: Random House, 1988.

Weiss, Harvey. *Machines and How They Work*. New York: Harper & Row, 1983.

Index